Rich
7 april 1995

Republic of Solitude

Poems 1984-1994

Republic of Solitude

Poems 1984-1994

Richard Greene

BREAKWATER

Breakwater
100 Water Street
P.O. Box 2188
St. John's, NF
A1C 6E6

*The publisher gratefully acknowledges the financial support of
the Canada Council, which has helped make this publication pos-
sible.*

*The publisher acknowledges the financial support of the Cultural
Affairs Division of the Department of Municipal and Provincial
Affairs, Government of Newfoundland and Labrador, which has
helped make this publication possible.*

Cover Photo: courtesy Dennis Minty.

Author Photo: Brian Sears

Canadian Cataloguing in Publication Data

Greene, Richard, 1961-
   Republic of solitude
   (Newfoundland poetry series)
   ISBN 1-55081-114-2
I. Title. II. Series.

PS8563.R43R46 1994 C811;.54   C94-950274-X
PR9199.3.G74R46   1994

Printed in Canada

Table of Contents

Stroller

I push the stroller down cobbled streets
As October turns each afternoon
To grey or brings on rain.
Sarah grows quiet amid the crowd
Watching herself in windows
Or staring down a corridor of legs.
Weathered stone over-hangs our walk
Dripping the past from parapets.
I mark time these afternoons,
Wheeling the future along before me.

Among Her Words

She bends first words across her tongue
And gives her universe a name.
First came "Ma" and "Ba" and "Da",
And then the fierce negation: "No",
With a stamping of her foot.
Now she finds a subtlety in things:
A "fl'r" is where you put your nose and smile;
A "bir'" will sing but flies when chased;
A "boot" will take you tramping in the yard.
And so each day she strives among her words
And draws with patience closer
To some full saying she desires.

Dressing

I dress my daughter for a day of cold:
The blouse embroidered with plump balloons,
The trousers with pockets for clips and coins,
The buckled shoes with toes a little scuffed,
The blue serge coat her mother also wore,
And then the woollen mitts she soon takes off
To touch the first cold wind that touches her.

Anno Domini

For Peter Levi

The day's light grows short through Autumn;
There is no call for secrecy or shade.
The leaves fall, lie crisp a while and loud
Where the foot falls. I never quite expect
The last warm day to be the last
Or the frost to solemnize the ground.
The ritual year is withering into hope
As a taper set in the whispering dark
Consumes a lifetime in its flame.
I think that no one is ever young,
We are born so close to decline.

Custom

The world is drifting further from this world,
And every hope is inwardly compelled
From nervousness and acts compounding noise
To strange exclusions and darkening surprise.

I imbibe new silence with every breath,
And my range of purpose grows less and less,
For clear beyond the customs of this heart,
My life is drifting endlessly apart.

English December

Thin mist rises from the gutters and grates.
Leaves hang limp from the season, dying late.
Beer cans float with swans on muddish water.
An old punt has rotted in the river.
English December is too soon for snow
Though razoring winds have steadily blown
The dead scraps of light from autumnal sense,
And low grey silences have grown immense.

Slush

December's fact, cold accustomed solitude,
The cold accustomed self, uncountable.
I walk in the mind of music I have loved
And of poets too potent to last.
I tread among the millions of December
Through salt and grit and the fumes of enterprise.
I am dreaming in my heart of God,
Waking to comets and the stars fallen.
I am lost in a cold circuit of streets;
The snow and the stars have melted in my hair.

Willa Cather

August sun and long fields of America,
Harvestable now in corn, wheat, or yams,
Recall the first incursions of an iron tip,
Strange tongues murmuring over crops,
Flesh furrowed, so much mingled under soil,
The sunflowers a ripening chronicle.

Waking

I wake in the beginning of light,
Earlier than history by an hour,
As darkness is chosen and unchosen
In the small volitions of an eye-lid.

I am born in the throat of the first bird
In an hour that will not perch or fly;
I am heard in a brief music of trees
Where no sound is lasting or ever lost.

The sky is rising in a body of light,
Blue with the first integrity of flame.
My low window fills with a chance of God:
I kindle countless mornings to an ash.

Utopia

I

An immense acreage of solitude.
No one has lived here
Or left more than a shadow
Among shrubs and stones.
The hill falls to water
And a carious rock:
Geology is a study of the spirit,
One place forming another
In the migrations of a continent.
I am always here
On a hillside of quartz and juniper,
A ridge over water
Where the whales blow and dive,
And the grounded ice-bergs topple
In a smoke of gulls.
This place is twenty years of me,
The stark coastland of a question.

Who dares learn such emptiness,
Contending with thoughts of ocean,
Or interiors yet a wilderness?
And learning, who dares forget?
The world is more populous than the soul:
There are hermits in Soho.
Europe will have a radioactive Summer
And tumours subsequently.
This morning as I prayed
Americans flew past in a transport plane
Perhaps too full of bombs for greeting.
I listen to my breath
And the machine that eats motor-cars
For breakfast;
They find nutrition in our old manoeuvres.
I am still listening to my breath,
I think that I am here.

III (Isaiah 22: 16-18)

What right have you here,
And what relatives have you here
For you to hew yourself
A tomb in this place?
See, Yahweh hurls you down,
Down with a single throw;
Then with a strong grip he grips you
And winds you up into a ball
And hurls you into an immense country.
There you will die.

IV

O my immense country of no place,
There is nowhere as strange as now.
I am alone in this acreage of breath,
Landscape of spruce, fir, clover, and rock,
A lifetime expiring somewhere worlds away.

Rain

The vacant hour has filled with rain.
The little girl goes indoors
And the orbit of her bicycle is over.
I think of big things in my life.
Naomi thinks of kinsman Boaz,
Sends Ruth to glean the darkness.
Am I right to listen to myself?
Prayer is watering the grass
With an emphatic gesture,
Threshing bells from handle bars
And sleeping among the shrubs.
This is a new place to live,
Exercising the right of bicycle
Over so many wet bricks.
The bells have poured out
Their ephah of sound
On a city that resembles dawn.
Naomi says the little girl
Will ride before the hour
When one cloud can recognize another.

Widowing

Imagine a death not my own,
The cycle of seasons excluding me,
A mystery in the fall of leaves
Or the hand of water on a rock,
The sky perishing among swallows,
The world dying as I grow strong.

Frost is a widowing of the Earth;
I thought I was dying in the smell of cold,
In the stature of the icy trees;
You are now my vast mortality,
Bride of compassion, and of snow.

House and Barn

One night a weight of snow would bring the roof
Into the house, onto the empty beds,
And the walls would lean in toward sleep,
The bowed timbers snore in their collapse.

And there was weather enough to do it,
The snow burning above the black water,
The ocean blown onto the island cliffs,
The seabirds sleeping on the back of storms.

Some nights a sudden wind wanted the barn,
And laid its hands on the rotten boards
To dance seduction back and forth till dawn,
Whispering away resistance to the fall.

I looked through a window into miles of fog,
Wondering when that world would break
And I not know what weather passed for dreams
In a bed where my first years grew cold.

Fragment

Dominican splendour, sweeping black and white
Along the hallways of a grey prison.
The angel is also claustrophobic:
The screw's delinquency, the will waiting
By a door, heaven is closed, the wind cold,
Razor wire along the high perimeter.
Palm Sunday, a procession over palms.

Swan

I have heard the swan dying in a voice,
The water running through years of music,
Too old for the reeds, for the floating bloom
Of a lily touched with the Moon's ambition.
I have heard that cane tapping upon the waves
Where great wings extend the soul's agony
And the long neck cannot lift its weight of song.
He walks on the water of his last years
And his poetry is all unknowing,
Recurrence of breath and cloud and shadow,
The swan's obsession with the floating stars.
He sings of water and the love of water
And the long rest under the willow's hair.

Landscapes

The sky is broad vacancy,
      Late but not yet stars.
The sun is flames, consuming, failing.
      White clouds become ash,
            A light breeze carrying them.
So day ends
      In a few elements,
            Purities of unknowing.
The light is level, orange, intense,
      Burning what must be
            Miles of water.

Temple and labyrinth,
      Fir trees, spruce trees, enclose
         A month of early rising
            Ten years past.
This was once a ploughed field,
      Of which two furrows remained.
Trees are taller now,
      And more have grown.

The land falls on three sides
    To pasture.
I stand on a grassy shoulder,
    Eyes follow the flesh of the land
        Into a haze of thorns,
            Then a forest of birch and maple,
                And one clear artery flowing.

Wind presses a long argument.
    The snow ponders.
A surface hardens
    To troughs and corrugations.
Stars generate so little light
    That edges of the wind
        Are never seen.

My Fourth Body

The morning stirs in our sleep
And we have dreamed a new sanity
Among waving limbs.

I give myself to this nurture
Growing flesh to cover the single hope
That swims in the heart's womb.

I live now in my fourth body,
Years and years of the will of God
Forming one child.

I will wake in child-birth
With pangs of the free act
I dare not choose.

Burial

I have buried Judas in the body of God.
His cold flesh lies under a hill that is God's breast,
His soul is breathing the long roots of history,
He will listen to movements of the world's decay,
For he has become like holy ground in Israel.

The lungs of Jesus are emptied of their last psalm,
And the world's slow cramp is loosened from limb to limb.
He is laid in the melting eye of God's desire,
Where the Earth has pondered him among all deep wounds
And followed his clay rising with a new embrace.

Elsewhere

I think of my worlds to come,
And I am walking in a landscape
Beyond memory or prediction,
A hillside entirely strange,
Among the audible silences,
Along a bodiless turf.
Who would become absolute elsewhere
Who started in flesh and bones,
In the lines on an infant's palm?
We come to ourselves unexpected
At the last,
As blossoms strangers to the stem,
Somewhere more than we imagined.

Isaiah 55: 11

"... so the word that goes from my mouth
does not return to me empty ..."

I am young and old and not of heaven;
My little becomes less though more is given.
A breath returns in secret thoughts of time
To a God for whose eternal mind
We are unknowing, we are dark unknown;
Somewhere he is praying to us alone,
Whose prayer is always to follow a breath
Through our burning tides of birth and death,
And we are the dark night of his deep soul,
A raw love, infinite and unconsoled.

I am young and old and not of heaven;
My little becomes less though more is given.
Breaths of my flesh, I count breaths from that fire,
Count them, respire, suspire, inspire, expire,
I count breaths of my flesh, breaths of his flesh,
Fire of my flesh, fire from him fresh,
Guttering, guttering always in time,
And never again in this world the fire of his mind.
Beyond the choices of a perfect love,
We love badly, love still, still we are loved,
Though breath is unfelt, that fire without flame,
Who has chosen never to be the same,
Or twice to love without new creation,
New fall, new prophets, new crucifixion,
To find new darkness in his darkened prayer,
The virtue of God to teach himself despair.

I am young and old and not of heaven;
His little becomes less, no more is given.
In my flesh I have breathed his last breaths,
I have counted one by one his slow deaths,
I have heard him gasp the thick syllables
Of a psalm, heard the slow bell ring knell
Upon knell in the season of his loss,
As the eyes of heaven closed on that cross,
The fire dead, the breath gone, the body cold,

Heaven breathing away the broken soul.
The silence of God's prayer is agony,
In silence he is weeping bitterly,
For he cannot rejoint the twisted bones
Of Christ after Christ who must die alone,
And all his love is less than he intends:
Compassion is unbearable in the end.

I am young and old and not of heaven;
My little becomes less though more is given.
He bears alone as I could never bear
The slow duration of a weary prayer;
It goes ages in flame, ages in ash,
Recurring visions from a distant past,
The heat of breathing, the cold of time,
And his eyes more perfect if they were blind;
He pities though he may not touch the pain,
Dissolution, lives that will not come again
Into this world which alone has taught life
To the red clay, the chipped edge of the stone knife,
As the universe gave one moment
For evolution, each breath and movement,
Before the accidental mass was stirred
And only pity might recall the world.
Human pity passes, it will always end
In a distraction; it will always spend
Its force in time, though he must suffer
Without hope of time: he will remember.

I am young and old and not of heaven:
I shall live for he has known me living;
He has torn down heaven for our sake.
We shall die, we shall die, we shall never wake
In this flesh or in these bones or in this world,
But in that mind we will be remembered,
Who remembers all things, God of the living,
Our little no less for all is given.

Independence

The edge of all the world,
An island, huge and empty,
Swimming in fog, worn away
By currents warm and cold,
And the memory of glaciers
Stripping soil from stone,
Oppression which preceded history.
Torn from North Africa,
Floating through its million years
Of independence, always at sea,
And the mystery of its inhabitants
Before the Beothucks, Brendan,
Or the Vikings,
Before empire or dominion,
The republic of its solitude.
To study politics in the stone,
Those hills which were volcanic,
The wrinkling and subsidence
Of an ageing land,
The palm tree becoming pine,
And still the wandering.

Dawn

A hay-field at dawn,
Sweat of the waking soil,
Smells of clover, smells of spruce,
A bird cracking the edges of night,
A dog running among birch trees.
The night sky pales from indigo
To grey, to blue,
As the moon hangs huge and low,
Contemplative through three colours of the sky.
I stand among stooped stalks of hay
Where the dew clusters
In loosely numbered mysteries;
I know more than myself at last,
Not discipline or dogma
To be abandoned or outworn,
But the colour of newness,
An intoxication of earliest blue,
Whose creeds are variable
In decades of the morning sun.

At Evening

At evening the lakes burn
And love like an orange flame
Covers itself in violet ash.
Over the barrens there is uncertain sleeping,
And the shambling moose
Ponders the slow stream,
Its winding intentions.
Far-off the low buzz of the highway
And the headlamps' glint
Suggest another place
Where love is possible.
Somewhere the embers of daylight
Keep warm,
And under darkness sustain their hunger.
The night is articulate,
Uttering stars,
And the querying owl
Cries out from its hidden bough.

Quieting of Titles

I

A question of title:
Who may claim the vacant space,
The serviceable plots of memory?
I shall name the pasture,
Mark its longitude and latitude
By minutes and seconds,
Situate it beside roadways and rivers,
Describe its customary uses,
And in affidavit name
Those who in former times
Had grazing there.
My history is topography,
But always a poor claim,
Purchase by gavelkind,
A handful of sod and soil
In lieu of documents
And the notary's seal.

II

Locus amoenus,
That place above the ocean
And that posture of the mind,
Looking to low cloud and grey water,
Seeking its own more distant origin
Among ships and islands,
Far-off Baccalieu.

III

The mind is a field dispossessed,
Place after place,
The one good place that is always lost.
The scythe whistles through August,
The silver prong and the hickory rake
The gathered bales at dusk.
The warm season flies up,
Wing upon wing,
Toward shelters of futurity.

IV

Eden
Bought and sold,
Real estate agents have trod, have trod,
And memory marks down gain and loss
In ruled columns,
Profit and oppression.
Never poor, and in no way oppressed,
I was only young.

V

Box-wire and barbed wire,
Marking the edge of property,
And the furthest edge of the secret world.
The child knows almost nothing of value;
His world consists of persons
And is merely intimate.

VI

It is not time for buying or for selling,
Or for the writing of papers that purport to buy or sell,
Or for the surveyor's gaze and the driven stake,
Marking the border between one life and another.
It is not time for any of these,
But for every thing that they are not.
Memory asserts its perpetual title
Over the world that it has lived in,
A field, a house, a barn, a grove of trees,
A childhood at the ocean's edge.
This lifetime I claim by adverse possession
And by the heart's customary access,
For this alone is refuge and solitude,
And this the place of my beginnings.

Hagia Sophia

An exact turning on a true centre,
Hagia Sophia,
Elaborate ballet unfolding time.

Whose lifted hand
Was the first fire of the universe,
Faint disturbance in the void.

Turn upon turn,
Leg and arm extending or coiling
Tight to the body.

The birth of systems,
Each violence gathered
In tragic symmetry of limbs.

What is spoken in gesture,
The vast movement among stars,
Spiralling implication.

And the smaller movement,
The closer turning,
A chosen world.

The Historian

The son of man writes letters by lamplight
In a house as old as the modern world;
He is almost at home in this place
In the shadows of quarried stone,
Among churches and monasteries,
Ancient libraries and colleges:
Bethlehem, Nazareth, and Paradise.
He disturbs by daylight
The intimate dust of old books,
Discovers new friendship among the dead
Who recorded their lives by accident
And sealed them in envelopes and red wax.
His study among the Essenes
Is one or two generations of the past
Approached by necromancy.
Thus he reads the apocalypse backwards
To some antique revelation
And discovers his own life foretold;
He reads then from the other direction
To know its end.

Oil-Barrel

Leaves enclose the mind
Where love unclothes itself,
Learns nakedness for the months of cold.
The wind fills with newspapers
And the leaves fall:
The year ends in whitened dark
Wandering barefoot under street-lamps.
Deep drifts gather and migrate
Across the last pages of the calendar;
Cars vanish under a falling sky.
At morning love stirs
A little comforted by daylight,
Shakes the night's snow from its limbs,
Sees an unbearable light
Refracted in icicles.
The snow-blower feeds on deciduous light
And trucks carry the morning away
In huge loads;
Hour by hour, the light is less.
The mind trudges in its bitter wind,
Following gaunt trees along a boulevard
Where their shadows fell.
The spirit lives only in numbness now,
At finger-tips where death is beginning:
The oil-barrel breathes flame
In an implacable dark.

Vanishing

The I diminishing, the eye grows clear,
And the self which spread like a cataract
Is lifted from the light of mid-day:
A wisp of cloud passes and death is near.

The shoreline folds upon itself, vanishes
From place to place, suggesting elsewhere
To the indifferent soul, and the gull
Flies low toward distances, perishes.

What is lifted up, broken by the fingers,
Is pure immortality once the self
Has rolled like a parchment from the sky:
Bread and wine, sunlight and seawater.

Allegiance

Politics is a bubbling at the source,
A sound where there are ears to hear it.
Inland a river gives birth to oceans
Soon enough, and the solitary places
Echo with true conversations.
My new world is begun in emptiness,
In the dereliction of old lives,
The silent houses and the fallen shacks
Of a dispersed people;
Their voices linger in the long grass,
Cry out from island to island,
Mutter endlessly over barrens.
Most just when most alone,
And most intimate from afar,
We learn compassion in raw wind
And in places of stone,
For the dead are no one's people
Except that they are heard and chosen.
We give them our world to inhabit
And they become our justice,
In each moment demanding return
And restitution for their bones:
Revolution begins only in dust,
In those untended graves
And their rain-washed wooden markers.
It is in the course of things
That I should go to them,
Visit their weathered hillsides,
Give over to them, voice for voice,
My world for another to be born,
And always it must begin with them,
Who are the politics of stony places,
Considered passion of the wilderness.

Thirteenth Night

I hoover up the rubble of Christmas,
Bright shreds of wrapping, carpeted biscuit crumbs,
Ornamental shards of a fallen angel,
Satsuma stems, red and green ends of string.
Now, the night after twelfth night, old Christmas
Growing older, the tree standing one last hour,
The house must turn to the simpler regime
Of school-going, work, library-delving,
Lives which will prosper through unfestive months
Of England's wet winter. Waybread in season:
The last dark fruit-cake one wise elf hid.

1000X

The profusion of the microscope:
I live with my wife and child
Among uncatalogued species of pleasure
That swim past like sudden tadpoles.
I can find no scale for the lesser miracles,
A domestic existence
Whose landscapes are a table-top,
A bed-sheet and a sink,
Whose horizons are paint and plaster,
And whose constellations
Are filaments minutely hung.
Love is a conversation in a water-drop.

Another Country

A nation which prospered by easy wars,
Woke to the booming dawn of a new world
And a competent foe, that lost England
Which blossoms only in obscurest stone
Of college chapels and village monuments.
Think of them and their century unspent,
The measured pace into no man's land,
The machine gun cutting down the future,
And one or two of the old surviving
On benches or in wheel-chairs,
Their age meant for a world that never lived,
Ypres and the Somme and the remembered dead.

The Years

For Cyril Pine

He asks, "Where do the years go?"
I wonder does he mean to be answered.
Tears gather like an avalanche
In old eyes, along the high slopes
Of innocence and regret,
And he turns his head away,
Gazes through a window toward the pasture
Where the last of his cows
Are grazing at dusk.
"Where do the years go?"
Some perhaps are in his hands,
In the knuckles and the broad thumbs,
And some perhaps are in his children,
And in the silent house they have left.
As for the rest,
There is only the night that comes on,
And the forgetting of love.
He falls into the privacy of his own death
Watching light vanish from the meadow,
Is silent, and turns again to the boy
Who fears such grief.
"Where do the years go?"
"Somewhere good I hope."
The old man had not expected an answer,
Nods again toward the darkness,
Whispers slowly,
"Somewhere good I hope."

Philosophers

Lonely outposts of the mind
Where armistice is undeclared,
And men in ragged puttees
Keep watch over the islands
Clutching spindly rifles
And their long rusted swords.
They have held to the code:
Bushido, a perfect scepticism.
Old age has not convinced them
That the sun-god of reason
Had his reasons to surrender.
They look upward for proofs
Of the old struggle,
And, seeing less than nothing,
They grieve for the lost Zero.

A Field of Statues

Places in the dream, I know them
As an exile from daylight.
I go down into that church
From which the south wall has vanished;
A huge and panoramic glass
Gives instead Flanders and the Somme
And still or again a time of war.
The statuary is elegiac and grandiose,
Grey stone eagles on towering pedestals,
And underbellies of a dozen stone horses,
The horses rearing and the gaze upward.
Two birds, flesh and feathers,
Fly through another window beside the altar,
Perch one above the other,
The tragic eagle and its comic friend.
I know this place and all its strangers.

The Resurrection

Ruth 3: 6-14

John 20: 1-18

She is the first witness of love's body,
Which time has buried and its true world reclaimed.
Roll back the stone to be redeemed by the lost body
Of the harvest lord, sleep at his feet
Whose sleep has changed him to a stranger.
He has taken the body from her mind
And set it treading the sunrise:
He has woken among the husks on the threshing floor,
And leaves her sleeping in the grey hours
Of gathering day.
He has harrowed Hell and threshed out the lights of heaven
To make good the claims of love:
And she goes from that moment of dust and paradise,
Into the fields of a time to come, rejoicing.
Mary Magdalene or Ruth the Moabitess,
In your eyes the bright vision that eludes us,
In your eyes the body of the resurrection.
I think of the Christ whom I have never seen:
He has risen before that hour when I might know him,
Ascended in the time of shadows;
And I look in the place where sleep changed him,
Where the bindings of this world lie like blown husks,
And the world's wit, rolled and separate,
Lies in death's corner that we might grieve for it.
In truth, this tomb is empty,
And the carcase of dear prophecy is silent on its slab,
But you, the witnesses of the soul's espousal
Out-wait me, counselled by angels.
Risen and lost, where along that road
At earliest morning
Has he gone, that now he will return to you,
Having paid your price of freedom?

Eagle

They came to this ascent,
Making their deaths in a labour of sunlight,
Climbing by ladder or stair into wind-blown heaven,
And Christ was an eagle perched in their hearts,
Tumbling towards his own incomparable vision
Beyond the stillness of his lost paradise.
In them the eagle has fallen from its height
And lies broken among shadows of the crevasse.
They came to this ascent in bright sunlight
Knowing it was their deaths they made by the eagle's wing,
Remembering his flight and his knowing eye,
And the wind-blown heaven of his prayers.
They climb by the innocence of his desire;
By that falling out of heaven's eyrie
He teaches flight to them in their slow rising,
And the soul nested at the world's high ledge
Is never safe: it is born for brokenness.
They have climbed the jagged edges of the world,
Looking for light among the cracks and fissures of the wind,
And the blood of Christ the eagle
Darkens their hands where they climb.
A mountain hermitage, the stylite's perch,
Athos and Meteora at a fatal precipice,
Places of the secret inward ascent:
Sharpened edges of clouds and cold naked light of the Sun,
The raw purity of the eagle's flight,
Granite and the God falling.

Spring 1992

Enter Spring, as this country's time goes out:
April, who comes with a simpleton's shout,
Is our betrayal of a sacred past —
All blossom swears the old has loved its last.

This new life comes as waste and afterthought,
For Earth, repeating deaths the soul forgot,
Consoles with a recurrence of despair,
Breathes out insulted love like poisoned air.

Island, whose justice withered under snow,
Turn now to watch that colder virtue go,
And I, who loved your bleak austerity,
Divorce my heart from this intensity.

Necropolis

City of my birth, love's necropolis,
I stand in sight of your profaned temple,
Whose towers, scaffolded, mark an oracle
Of dry visions, a vipered paradise.

Your helmeted men purge out histories
With a poisonous wash; the old bell
Is silent in its unholy steeple,
As stone by stone you disown your mysteries.

I speak now to your most sentient core,
Knowing it dead, and what has died in it,
The ancient soul you never can restore;

That passion in each stone made intimate,
A prophet's waste of blood and labour,
To this my heart is chained, Christ's idiot.

The Swimmers

Along the rippled water of bodies
One life into another disappears,
For the swimmers have dissolved with their strokes,
Thigh upon thigh and mouth pressed against mouth:
They are the river's private narrative,
The undoing of selfhood in true desire,
The winding bed and tributary limbs
Of lovers striving toward some ocean,
The perfect torrent of their single stream.

The Long Retreat

It is grazing land in Autumn.
The field stretches off half a mile and ends in clouds
Of thorn at the edge of maple, birch, and poplar.
Somewhere past what I can see is the slow river
That runs in summer under leaves, and runs now
Among stark shadows of these high and naked boughs.
This is the long retreat, thirty days to live out
Christ's mortality in meditation and prayer,
Seeking the child and the man in the still waters
Of my imagining, his face and his flesh
In the dust of memory and also in the dust
I am to be.

I walk over the acres of dry frost
In the hours that are not marked for prayer,
Listening to the fall of sunlight in November,
The crisp solitudes of farmland and woodland
Which live in the ear all these winters past.
How little came of my imaginings and how much;
Flesh and blood that I remember now as time and place,
This earth, these trees, those years ago,
                    A path I did not take.

Valediction

While you live there is time enough for valediction,
But these last months are all of time for you,
Measured in shortening breaths,
Where ripened tumours crowd you into air.

Flesh and bone are not space enough
For this farewell or this beginning;
I will greet you in your silent journey,
Your breath of starlight through this sacred air.

Extinction

Motion within motion,
Deep movement in the darkest waters:
It is the primal wit in the sea's heart,
This creature that journeys out its years
And propagates its simple appetites
At the ocean's floor.
The curve and sway
Of flesh and bone and fin,
Infinite recurrence,
And the instinct of a million generations
Schooled in movement only:
It cannot name its own passion for continuance
Or know some place as destiny
Where the wandering ends.

Greed is an evolutionary triumph,
Spawning new evils in humankind
That were less than instinct
In lesser life.

The codfish,
Who knows nothing but its way,
Perishes in nets and mesh,
Sunken mazes of unintelligible desire.

Glass

Liturgy in the Summer dusk,
Huge saints of leaded glass
Aflame in the falling light.
Memory contains this night
In itself,
And again in the recollection
Of itself:
Such hours of fervency
Under the wakened gaze
Of Winter's dull patriarchs.
This evening five years ago
And fifteen:
Between them,
The years of blackened glass,
The journey from self to self
In the half lights of providence,
And now, again,
The dusk that enfolds them in fire.

Mist

Some only self breathes silence from sea-mist,
And in grey light elusive hopes persist,
Nameless and raw his sudden appetite,
Flame of inwardness, emptiness, and night.

What alone in him is living goes out
To futures that parch the tongue like drought,
Toward a desert that the soul requires,
Or salt on stones, cold waves, its last desires.

Acknowledgement

The third section of "Utopia", quoting verses from Isaiah, is not a new translation. Apart from a minor alteration I have made, it is taken directly from *The Jerusalem Bible*. Other quotations from the Bible are also from this translation, and I gratefully acknowledge my debt to its translators and publishers.

I would also like to express gratitude to the editors of *Poetry Canada Review*, *Grail*, *Acumen Magazine*, *The Newfoundland Quarterly*, *Tickleace*, and The Oxford University Poetry Society Broadsheet, in which publications some of these poems have already appeared.